THE SILENT TRACK: AN EXPLORATION OF ABANDONED RAILWAYS

Chronicles of Deserted Tracks and Their Ghost Trains

D.R. T Stephens

S.D.N Publishing

CONTENTS

Title Page

Copyright

General Disclaimer   1

Chapter 1: Echoes of the Past: Introduction to Abandoned   3
Railways

Chapter 2: The Golden Era: The Heyday of Railways and Their   6
Subsequent Decline

Chapter 3: Nature's Reclamation: How Earth Retakes Deserted   9
Tracks

Chapter 4: Ghostly Stations: A Look at Abandoned Train   12
Stations Around the World

Chapter 5: The Legends of Ghost Trains: Myths, Tales, and   15
Supernatural Stories

Chapter 6: Economic Shifts: The Role of Changing   18
Economies in Railway Desertion

Chapter 7: Battle Scars: War and Its Impact on Railways   21

Chapter 8: Rails to Trails: Transforming Old Tracks into   24
Recreational Paths

Chapter 9: Notable Train Wrecks and Their Everlasting   27
Marks

Chapter 10: Artistic Expressions: Graffiti and Art in   30
Abandoned Stations

Chapter 11: Tales from the Tracks: Personal Narratives from   33
Railway Workers

Chapter 12: The Environmental Impact: Nature's Recovery   36
and Environmental Benefits

Chapter 13: Preserving History: Efforts to Protect and   40
Maintain Deserted Railways

Chapter 14: The Allure of Urban Exploration: Risks and   44
Rewards

Chapter 15: Cinematic Rails: Abandoned Railways in Film   48
and Television

Chapter 16: Photographic Journeys: Capturing the Essence of   52
Ghost Trains

Chapter 17: The Role of Politics: Government Decisions and   56
Their Consequences for Railways

Chapter 18: Railway Ghost Towns: Communities Built and   60
Dissolved Around Trains

Chapter 19: Future Prospects: Potential Reuses for   64
Abandoned Tracks and Stations

Chapter 20: Safety Measures: Precautions for Railway   68
Explorers

Chapter 21: Rebirth and Revival: Stories of Deserted   72
Railways Brought Back to Life

Chapter 22: Farewell to the Silent Tracks: Reflecting on the   76
Legacy of Abandoned Railways

THE END   79

GENERAL DISCLAIMER

This book is intended to provide general information to the reader on the topics covered. The author and publisher have made every effort to ensure that the information herein is accurate and up-to-date at the time of publication. However, they do not warrant or guarantee the accuracy, completeness, adequacy, or currency of the information contained in this book. The author and publisher expressly disclaim any liability or responsibility for any errors or omissions in the content herein.

The information, guidance, advice, tips, and suggestions provided in this book are not intended to replace professional advice or consultation. Readers are strongly encouraged to consult with an appropriate professional for specific advice tailored to their situation before making any decisions or taking any actions based on the content of this book.

The views and opinions expressed in this book are those of the author and do not necessarily reflect the official policy or position of any other agency, organization, employer or company.

The author and publisher are not responsible for any actions taken or not taken by the reader based on the information, advice, or suggestions provided in this book. The reader is solely responsible for their actions and the consequences thereof.

This book is not intended to be a source of legal, business, medical or psychological advice, and readers are cautioned to seek the services of a competent professional in these or other areas of expertise.

All product names, logos, and brands are property of their respective owners. All company, product and service names used in this book are for identification purposes only. Use of these names, logos, and brands does not imply endorsement.

Readers of this book are advised to do their own due diligence when it comes to making decisions and all information, products, services and advice that have been provided should be independently verified by your own qualified professionals.

By reading this book, you agree that the author and publisher are not responsible for your success or failure resulting from any information presented in this book.

CHAPTER 1: ECHOES OF THE PAST: INTRODUCTION TO ABANDONED RAILWAYS

The romance of the railways is an evergreen affair. Throughout history, the allure of trains chugging along tracks, piercing through countryside vistas, and whistling a haunting tune has captured the imagination of many a traveler, artist, and writer. But what happens when these very symbols of movement and connection come to a grinding halt, forgotten by the world? They become silent witnesses to the tales of days gone by, echoing stories of bustling platforms, joyous journeys, tearful goodbyes, and economic landscapes that changed faster than the tracks themselves.

To many, an abandoned railway is simply a rusty relic of the past. But to the keen observer, it's a labyrinth of stories waiting to be discovered. It's the ivy-covered station that once echoed with laughter but now stands still in silent contemplation. The overturned train car may have once witnessed an illicit romance or two. And the track, now covered in autumn leaves, which used to glisten in the sun, guiding trains to destinations unknown.

The history of rail travel is replete with tales of the indomitable human spirit and the relentless march of progress. As steam-powered behemoths gave way to sleek diesel engines, and as small regional stops turned into bustling metropoles, the landscape of the railways underwent tremendous change. Some tracks found themselves at the heart of these changes, adapting and thriving, while others found themselves overshadowed and redundant.

Now, one might wonder, why did these tracks fall silent? Ah, dear reader, it's not a simple tale of obsolescence. For every abandoned railway, there's a complex web of social, economic, and political reasons. The oil crisis, the rise of the automobile, wars, regional politics, and sometimes just the sheer inevitability of progress have played their part. Some tracks were abandoned for a reason as mundane as a more efficient route being found, while others bore the brunt of geopolitical upheavals.

Yet, amidst this somber reflection, there's a silver lining. Abandoned doesn't necessarily mean forgotten. These silent tracks, in their decay, have a beauty that's both melancholic and inspiring. Nature, in its infinite wisdom, often reclaims these spaces, intertwining rusted rails with wildflowers, creating a landscape that's an enchanting blend of the industrial and the natural. Photographers, history buffs, and urban explorers find themselves drawn to these places, each looking for a different story, each leaving with a unique memory.

So, let's embark on this journey together, traversing the forgotten tracks, the ghostly stations, and the lost tales. Along the way, we'll unearth the legends of phantom trains, marvel at nature's tenacity to reclaim, delve into the economic machinations that led to the desertion of these tracks, and, hopefully, discover a part of ourselves in these rusted rails and crumbling platforms.

Because you see, while these tracks might be silent, they're anything but voiceless. And as we journey through the pages of this book, I invite you to listen, really listen, to the echoes of the past. For in them, you might just find the future. And who knows, perhaps somewhere along the way, we might even awaken some of these silent tracks from their deep slumber.

So, grab your ticket, secure your luggage, and let's embark on a voyage through time, history, and the silent tracks that bear testimony to both. All aboard!

CHAPTER 2: THE GOLDEN ERA: THE HEYDAY OF RAILWAYS AND THEIR SUBSEQUENT DECLINE

The pages of history are bursting with instances of humans' tireless pursuit of progress. Like star-crossed lovers, we humans have forever been enchanted by movement, by the idea of traveling great distances, and by the promise of what lies beyond the horizon. And of all our pursuits, few compare in scale, ambition, or poetry to the rise of the railways.

The Steam-Powered Revolution

Our tale begins with the advent of the steam engine. Picture, if you will, a time in the early 19th century when the world first witnessed trains powered by steam puffing through verdant countryside, forging connections between cities and towns. With each turn of the wheel and each plume of smoke, these metallic marvels declared the beginning of an era that would reshape continents.

The steam engine, with its ability to pull heavy loads over long distances, was nothing short of revolutionary. No longer would humans be reliant on the whims of horses or the unpredictable nature of waterways. The train, with its rhythmic chugging and reassuring predictability, soon became the emblem of modernity.

An Era of Expansion

As the 19th century wore on, this 'Golden Era' of railways saw an unprecedented surge in track-laying. From the English countryside to the vast expanses of the American West, rails became the new arteries of burgeoning empires. These were not just means of transportation; they were tools of colonization, of economic boom, and of cultural exchange. The Trans-Siberian Railway, the Orient Express, the Pacific Railroad - each a testimony to human ingenuity, each a chapter in the saga of progress.

Stations turned into bustling hubs of activity, where businessmen jostled with tourists, where heartfelt reunions took place alongside tearful farewells. It was a time of prosperity, of movement, of an ever-shrinking world.

Signals of Change

But as with all golden eras, this one, too, began to wane. The 20th century brought with it challenges the railways hadn't anticipated. The two World Wars significantly impacted the industry, with tracks and stations often becoming theaters of conflict or strategic targets.

Yet, even as peace returned, the railways faced a new contender – the automobile. With the rise of personal vehicles and a network of roads, the lure of personal mobility began to overshadow the communal experience of train travel. Planes further reshaped the way we perceived distances. The convenience of air travel and the thrill of a road trip offered a contrast to the stately pace of trains.

The Inevitable Decline

By the mid-20th century, many rail lines, once the pride of nations, began to see a decline in their fortunes. Urbanization and economic considerations meant that some tracks, especially those in remote areas, were deemed unviable. Railways, once seen as symbols of progress, now bore the brunt of it.

The decline wasn't uniform. While some tracks faded into obscurity, others were repurposed. Some found new life as heritage routes, while others were dismantled, their metal reincarnated into newer infrastructures.

But for the tracks that were left behind, the departure was never truly complete. The trains may have stopped, but their memories lingered, echoing tales of a time when steam, steel, and ambition converged to define an era.

Ah, dear reader, the golden era of railways is a tale of highs and lows, of roaring engines and silent tracks. But as we delve deeper into these chronicles, remember that every rusted nail, every overgrown platform has a story, a story of humanity's boundless dream to connect, to traverse, and to conquer. All aboard the time machine, for the journey has only just begun!

CHAPTER 3: NATURE'S RECLAMATION: HOW EARTH RETAKES DESERTED TRACKS

In the heart of a dense forest, where sunlight barely seeps through the thick canopy above, a faint glimmer of metal can sometimes be spotted beneath the carpet of moss and leaves. Here, amongst the whispering trees, lies a once proud railway track. It's a scene that might be straight out of a fairytale - the Earth gently reclaiming what was once hers.

Nature's Gentle Embrace

Contrary to popular belief, nature isn't vindictive or retaliatory. She's patient. When humans desert their infrastructures, nature doesn't pounce instantly. Rather, she begins a gentle dance of reclamation.

Initially, the tiniest of weeds might sprout between the wooden railway ties. Rain, wind, and time work their erosive magic, creating cracks for seeds to lodge and germinate. Before you know it, saplings take root, drawn to the sunlight and unfazed by the metal rails.

A Flourishing Ecosystem

What's particularly poetic about these reclaimed railways is the diversity of life they host. They become linear oases. Wildflowers bloom in a riot of colors, offering nectar to butterflies and bees. Birds build nests in the crevices, while small mammals scuttle beneath the dense undergrowth, navigating the old tracks like highways.

There's something deeply moving about watching a deer graze beside rusting rail lines or witnessing a family of foxes make their den in an abandoned signal box. Nature, it seems, has a penchant for irony.

Beyond the Flora and Fauna

The reclamation isn't merely aesthetic. Over time, these tracks play a vital role in local ecosystems. They serve as green corridors, allowing wildlife to traverse landscapes fragmented by human development. By offering shelter and sustenance, they ensure the survival of myriad species.

Moreover, the slow decomposition of wooden sleepers and rusting of tracks release minerals back into the soil, enriching it and ensuring a fertile ground for future generations of plants.

Mysterious Elegance

But perhaps the most enchanting aspect of these reclaimed railways is their aesthetic allure. There's a profound serenity in seeing tracks enveloped in a cascade of ivy or stations with roofs blanketed in wildflowers. It's as if the world has stumbled upon the intersection of human ambition and nature's resilience.

For photographers and explorers, these spots offer a canvas like no other - where the industrial meets the organic, where decay intertwines with growth.

The Philosophical Perspective

If one were to wax philosophical (and why not, given the poetic surroundings?), these reclaimed railways offer profound insights into the transient nature of human endeavors. They serve as silent testimonies to the cyclical nature of existence - of rise, decline, and renewal.

For while our trains might have moved on to other tracks, the trails they left behind are far from lifeless. They pulse with a different kind of energy, one that's quieter but no less vibrant.

So, the next time you come across an overgrown track or a moss-covered platform, pause for a moment. Listen to the whispers of the wind and the rustle of the leaves. They tell tales of a time when locomotives roared, but they also sing praises of the world's eternal dance of rebirth and reclamation. A dance where nature always leads, and we, despite our grand designs, are but fleeting partners.

CHAPTER 4: GHOSTLY STATIONS: A LOOK AT ABANDONED TRAIN STATIONS AROUND THE WORLD

In the realm of forgotten railways, it isn't just the tracks that hold secrets; the stations do too. These sentinel structures, once bustling hubs of life, have turned into eerie, silent witnesses of time's relentless march. But even in their quiet decay, they whisper tales from the past. So, shall we board this ghost train of memories and journey through some of the world's most hauntingly beautiful stations?

1. Canfranc International Railway Station, Spain

Sprawling over the Pyrenees, the Canfranc International Railway Station could easily be mistaken for a royal palace. Opened in 1928, it was one of Europe's largest stations. But by 1970, it was shut, leaving behind a vast, ornate structure that now plays host to stray cats and the echoes of past conversations. Rumor has it spies traded secrets here during World War II. The station might be silent now, but oh, if those walls could talk!

2. Michigan Central Station, USA

Detroit's grandiose Michigan Central Station, with its towering pillars and vast windows, was once the tallest rail station in the world. Built in 1913, it saw thousands pass through its doors daily. But as automotive travel gained traction (pun intended!), the station's importance waned. By 1988, the last train departed, leaving an architectural marvel at the mercy of time and vandals. Recently, efforts have been made to restore it, but its ghostly charm remains intact.

3. Gudum Railway Station, Denmark

Tucked away amidst Denmark's picturesque landscapes is Gudum Railway Station. Unlike the grand stations, Gudum's charm lies in its quaintness. Closed in 1971, it now seems like a setting straight out of a Hans Christian Andersen tale, where one half expects to see fairies flitting about.

4. Kayas Train Station, Turkey

Legends surround Kayas, an abandoned train station near Ankara. Locals speak of a bride who waits eternally for her lover's return. On misty nights, some claim they've seen her spectral figure near the tracks, her white gown shimmering in the moonlight. Whether true or not, there's no denying the haunting allure of this forsaken spot.

5. Charleroi Train Station, Belgium

Once a symbol of Belgium's thriving coal industry, the Charleroi station now stands as a monument to an era gone by. As the coal mines closed, so did the station's importance. Today, nature paints its art on the decaying walls, and moss-covered platforms wait for passengers who will never come.

6. Jukkasjärvi Station, Sweden

Deep inside the Arctic Circle lies the ghostly Jukkasjärvi Station. Built to transport ice from the Torne River, its usage dwindled with the advent of modern refrigeration techniques. Today, in the chilling Arctic silence, it's said you can hear the faint laughter of workers and the distant chug of trains from yesteryears.

Taking Stock

These stations, scattered across continents, might differ in architecture and history, but they share a common thread — a testament to human ambition, resilience, and the inevitable passage of time. They're more than just brick and mortar; they're chronicles of lives lived, farewells bid, and stories spun.

It's funny, isn't it? For places that are associated with departures, these abandoned stations have a way of drawing people in. Maybe it's their silent dignity or the tantalizing mysteries they hold. Or perhaps, it's the allure of a world that once was, where steam billowed, whistles blew, and life pulsated.

For the intrepid explorer, these stations are portals to another time. So, the next time you stumble upon one, pause. Listen to its tales. For in its silence lies a cacophony of memories just waiting to be discovered. All aboard?

CHAPTER 5: THE LEGENDS OF GHOST TRAINS: MYTHS, TALES, AND SUPERNATURAL STORIES

Gather round, dear reader, and lend an ear, for we're about to delve deep into the enigmatic world of phantom locomotives and their spectral cargo. Yes, ghost trains! These aren't just the spooky tales told around campfires but legends and myths that have persisted through the ages, becoming as much a part of local folklore as they are enigmatic tales of the railway world.

1. The Phantom Express of Lincolnshire, England

In the misty moors of Lincolnshire, tales abound of a phantom train steaming across the tracks, whistle-blowing, only to vanish into thin air. Dating back to the late 19th century, many weary traveler has reported this ghostly apparition. Local legends suggest it's the restless spirit of a train that met with a tragic accident, forever destined to retrace its final journey.

2. The Silverpilen (Silver Arrow) of Stockholm, Sweden

In the depths of Stockholm's metro system, a silver train without advertisements, aptly named Silverpilen, is said to occasionally pick up passengers. Those who board it find themselves in stations long forgotten or sometimes never reach their destinations at all. Some say it's a test train, others a phantom of old railways. Either way, many locals prefer waiting for the next train than risk a journey on the mysterious Silverpilen.

3. The St. Louis Light, Saskatchewan, Canada

On an old, unused track north of St. Louis in Saskatchewan, a mysterious light can be seen bobbing in the distance, often mistaken for an oncoming train. But there's no train on those tracks, not for years. Local tales link the light to a railway conductor who tragically lost his head in an accident and now searches for it with a lantern in hand.

4. The Ghost Train of Bostian Bridge, North Carolina, USA

Every year, on the anniversary of its fatal crash in 1891, it's said that a phantom train can be seen hurtling off the Bostian Bridge in Statesville, only to disappear into the creek below. Witnesses have reported hearing the anguished screams of passengers and the ear-splitting crash, sending shivers down their spines.

5. The Funeral Train of Abraham Lincoln, USA

One of the most legendary ghost trains in history is the funeral train of Abraham Lincoln. It's said that every year, on the anniversary of Lincoln's death, his funeral train can be seen on its route from Washington, D.C., to Springfield, Illinois. The phantom train, draped in black with dim lanterns, is a chilling reminder of a nation's mourning.

Tales as Old as the Tracks

From the outback of Australia to the heartlands of Europe, almost every rail network has its own tale of a phantom train or a haunted track. Are these mere myths spawned from collective memories of tragedies? Or perhaps there's something inherently haunting about the idea of a massive, powerful machine, now silent and invisible, yet still making its presence felt.

Maybe these tales persist because trains, in all their glory, symbolize journeys. And what's a more eternal journey than that of the afterlife? But whether you're a skeptic or a believer, one thing's for certain: these tales add another layer of mystique to the already enigmatic world of abandoned railways.

So, the next time you find yourself near a deserted track on a still night, strain your ears. Perhaps you'll hear the distant chug of a long-gone locomotive or the faint whistle of a train that's not there. And just for a moment, you might find yourself suspended between the realms of the living and the legends of the past. All aboard the ghost express!

CHAPTER 6: ECONOMIC SHIFTS: THE ROLE OF CHANGING ECONOMIES IN RAILWAY DESERTION

"Follow the money," they say, and you'll find the answer. If we chase the tracks of many of these abandoned railways, their destiny, more often than not, has been dictated by the shifting sands of global economies. As lovely as the imagery of ghostly trains and romantic tales of deserted rails can be, there's a pragmatic side to this story - and it's all about the cash, commerce, and coal mines.

1. Boom and Bust: Coal Mines and Railways

Coal was once the lifeblood of many communities, especially during the industrial revolution. Railways sprouted like veins across landscapes, vital for transporting coal to hungry cities and factories. But as mines ran dry or became unprofitable, the tracks leading to them lost their purpose. Towns that thrived turned into relics of a bygone era and the rails? Silent.

2. The Rise of Road Networks and Automobiles

Henry Ford might not have anticipated it, but the Model T was a game-changer. As road networks expanded and the appeal of personal cars grew, many short-distance railway routes faced stiff competition. "Why take the train when you can drive?" became the catchphrase of an era, leading to many local railway lines' gradual phasing out.

3. Globalization and the Seafaring Giants

Globalization transformed how goods are transported. Massive container ships could carry the load of hundreds of trains, making them a more economical option for international trade. Ports expanded, but many local railway lines connecting inland factories to smaller docks became obsolete in the face of this sea change.

4. Air Travel: The Sky's No Longer the Limit

Passenger trains had their heyday, whisking folks from city to city at unmatched speeds. But then, along came the jumbo jets, shrinking our world. Long-distance trains couldn't compete with the speed of air travel, and several iconic railway routes faded into history.

5. Changing Urban Patterns: From Downtowns to Suburbs

As cities grew and people began moving to the suburbs, downtown train stations saw fewer footfalls. Urban planning now centered around highways and roads, leading to a decline in inner-city rail networks in favor of metro systems or buses.

6. The High Cost of Maintenance

It's not cheap maintaining hundreds of miles of track, especially if they're not turning a profit. With declining passengers or freight, many railway companies faced a tough choice: invest heavily in maintenance or let the tracks go. For many, the latter was the only feasible option.

Economics: The Unsung Hero (or Villain)

While ghost stories and legends might be more enchanting, the reality is that many of our beloved railways were claimed not by phantoms but by fiscal policy, economic downturns, or technological advancements. It's a classic case of 'adapt or perish.' Some railways adapted, transforming into tourist attractions or heritage lines, while others... well, they found their way into our book.

But there's a silver lining. Abandoned railways, though born out of economic downturns or shifts, now offer a unique glimpse into history, ecology, and even urban planning. They stand as silent witnesses to the ever-evolving narrative of progress and change.

So, the next time you walk along a deserted track, remember beneath those rusted lines lies a rich tapestry of tales – of booms, busts, world fairs, world wars, and the relentless march of technology. Indeed, every silent track has its story, and often, it's a lesson in economics. A penny (or a track) for your thoughts?

CHAPTER 7: BATTLE SCARS: WAR AND ITS IMPACT ON RAILWAYS

Amidst the reverberating tales of deserted tracks and silent stations, a louder, graver echo haunts many rails: the drums of war. The conflict has left an indelible mark on the railway networks, altering their destinies and, in some cases, muting their once boisterous voices forever. Let's explore the deep trenches of history to understand how the tracks have both facilitated wars and become their victims.

1. Rails in the Midst of Conflict

World War I and II saw railways playing a pivotal role. They transported troops, ammunition, and essentials, proving to be the arteries that kept the war machine pulsating. Unfortunately, their importance made them primary targets for enemy forces. The result? Many railway infrastructures, from bridges to stations, were bombed or sabotaged.

2. The Trains That Carried Hope... and Despair

Wartime trains have stories of both hope and despair. They transported soldiers to the fronts, evoking teary farewells, and later brought back the wounded, evoking somber homecomings. Not all trains bore signs of hope, though; some became symbols of humanity's darkest hours, like those leading to concentration camps.

3. Reconstruction and Abandonment

After the smoke of battle cleared, nations were left with the daunting task of rebuilding. While some railway lines were restored to their former glory, many others, scarred and damaged beyond feasible repair, were left behind, a somber reminder of the conflict.

4. Cold War: Iron Curtains and Iron Rails

The Cold War introduced a different type of conflict, one not of direct battles but of ideological divides. Railways were sometimes severed due to political tensions, leading to tracks that abruptly ended at borders or 'iron curtains,' creating silent zones in the midst of geopolitical storms.

5. Tunneling through Adversity: Underground Rails

Wars often prompted innovations, including underground railways. Some tunnels and subterranean tracks were constructed for strategic purposes, ensuring the safe and stealthy transport of resources. Post-conflict, some of these were abandoned, their underground passages becoming historical catacombs.

6. Emotional Baggage: War Memorials on Tracks

Many abandoned stations and tracks have been converted

into memorials and museums commemorating the events that transpired. These transformed spaces serve as poignant reminders, making sure the tales of valor, sacrifice, and loss are never forgotten.

Chugging Through History

War has a profound way of changing landscapes, both geographically and emotionally. Railways, being crucial infrastructures, often bore the brunt of these conflicts. While some tracks resurrected, phoenix-like, from the ashes of war, others remain as battle scars, silent yet screaming of the tales they've witnessed.

So, the next time you wander on a deserted track or encounter an old railway bridge with marks of a bygone battle, pause and ponder. Behind every rusted rail and crumbled station could be stories of heroes, tales of love in the time of war, or maybe just the strategic decisions of generals long gone. But one thing's for sure: wars may have silenced these tracks, but they've amplified their histories.

CHAPTER 8:
RAILS TO TRAILS:
TRANSFORMING
OLD TRACKS INTO
RECREATIONAL PATHS

The allure of the abandoned track is undeniable. Where once the clatter of train wheels and the hiss of steam punctuated the air, silence now prevails. Yet, there's an undeniable romance in repurposing these forgotten arteries of transportation. Across the globe, derelict train routes are being transformed into recreational paths, ensuring that even in their silence, these tracks continue to bring joy.

1. The Beginning of a Movement

The 'Rails-to-Trails' movement began as a humble initiative, with communities recognizing the potential of deserted tracks as public pathways. By the late 20th century, these transformed routes began to dot landscapes, offering scenic byways for pedestrians, cyclists, and even horse riders.

2. Breathing New Life

The transformation from rail to trail isn't just about paving over old tracks. It's a deliberate and artistic endeavor, marrying history with contemporary use. Interpretive signs, benches from reclaimed sleepers, and station-themed rest stops all ensure that the railway's legacy remains palpable.

3. The Benefits of the Switch

While the charm of a ghost train is hard to replace, these new recreational paths offer their own set of rewards. They promote health and fitness, offer safe corridors for non-motorized transportation, and even provide economic boosts to adjacent communities. Plus, they're eco-friendly!

4. Iconic Rails-to-Trails Transformations

The High Line in New York is a perfect example. What was once an elevated rail track is now an urban oasis, blooming with native plants and bustling with life, all while offering breathtaking views of Manhattan's skyline.

Another trail worth a tip of the conductor's cap is The Katy Trail in Missouri. Spanning nearly 240 miles, it stands as the longest rail-trail conversion in the USA, showcasing the sheer potential of such projects.

5. Global Tracks Following Suit

This isn't merely an American phenomenon. From Australia's Bellarine Rail Trail to the U.K.'s Monsal Trail, countries worldwide are jumping on the 'rail-to-trail' bandwagon, proving that the love for repurposed tracks is universal.

6. Challenges on the Path

Transitioning from a railway to a recreational path isn't always smooth. Land ownership issues, environmental concerns, and the challenge of maintaining the trail's historical essence can often derail the best-laid plans. But as many successful trails show, where there's a will, there's a way!

All Aboard the Greenway Express!

As we wander these serene paths, it's heartening to see that while trains no longer traverse these tracks, they're far from forgotten. The whistle may have ceased, but in its place, the laughter of children, the chatter of families, and the soft hum of bicycle wheels keep the tracks alive. It's a testament to human ingenuity: even in abandonment, we find a way to craft joy. So, strap on those walking shoes or pump up those bike tires—there's a rail trail waiting to be explored and trust us, it's a journey worth taking.

CHAPTER 9: NOTABLE TRAIN WRECKS AND THEIR EVERLASTING MARKS

Trains, with their majestic allure, have shaped the world's history in countless ways. But along with tales of grandeur and progress, there lurk stories of unfortunate mishaps. Some train wrecks, catastrophic in their time, have imprinted themselves on the tracks and, even in their aftermath, serve as grim reminders of both human ambition and vulnerability.

1. The Tacoma Bridge Disaster - 1940

Let's begin with a spectacle that wasn't purely a train disaster but certainly involved one. The Tacoma Narrows Bridge in Washington State famously collapsed under strong winds a mere four months after its opening. While thankfully no humans perished, a train car was tragically sent into the chilly depths of the Tacoma Narrows strait.

2. The Great Train Wreck of 1918 - Nashville

On a fateful morning in July, two passenger trains collided head-on near Nashville, Tennessee, resulting in a death toll of over 100. It remains one of the deadliest rail accidents in U.S. history. The cause? A mere oversight in communication.

3. The Quintinshill Rail Disaster - 1915

Moving across the pond, the Quintinshill Rail Disaster stands as Britain's deadliest train accident. Resulting from a series of unfortunate errors, two passenger trains collided with a parked troop train. The subsequent fires led to the loss of around 226 lives, many of whom were soldiers heading to the battlefront of World War I.

4. The Gaisal Train Disaster - 1999

Asia isn't untouched by the specter of rail disasters. The Gaisal Train Disaster in India saw two trains collide in the dead of night, igniting the onboard gas cylinders. The explosion and fire took the lives of at least 285 people.

5. The Memories They Carve

While these disasters are tragic, the echoes they leave behind are profound. Memorials, safety reforms, and literature spawned from these incidents ensure that the lessons, and more importantly, the lives lost, aren't forgotten.

6. The Silver Lining: Safety Reforms

There's a saying: "From the ashes, a phoenix rises." In the context of rail disasters, the phoenix often takes the shape of safety innovations. Each major accident led to introspection and an overhaul of existing safety protocols. Advanced signaling systems, better track maintenance, and improved communication methods are just a few of the myriad improvements made in the aftermath of these catastrophes.

7. The Ghostly Echoes on the Tracks

Some claim that on dark, silent nights, the tracks still whisper tales of the bygone era, echoing with the sounds of steam, steel, and sometimes, the spectral cries from tragedies of yore. Abandoned tracks, in particular, seem to hold on to these memories tighter than most, making them intriguing, if not a tad eerie, for explorers.

In winding down our journey through these notable train wrecks, it's essential to note that while they signify moments of human error and tragedy, they also exemplify our capacity to learn, innovate, and above all, to remember. The silent tracks might not reverberate with the clamor of locomotives anymore, but the stories they carry are as poignant and significant as ever. So, the next time you find yourself near an abandoned track, pause for a moment, listen closely, and you might just catch a fleeting echo from the past.

CHAPTER 10: ARTISTIC EXPRESSIONS: GRAFFITI AND ART IN ABANDONED STATIONS

Ah, the artful dance between decay and expression. Abandoned railways and stations, those silent sentinels of the past, have often become the canvases for modern-day artists, capturing the vibrancy of the present while paying homage to bygone days. Let's embark on a visual journey where paint meets rust and where every graffiti tag whispers tales from the silent tracks.

1. A Canvas Like No Other

As railroads ceased operations, their stations and sidings turned into empty vast expanses, devoid of life but brimming with potential. It didn't take long for artists armed with spray cans and dreams to recognize the artistic opportunities these spaces presented.

2. From Vandalism to Vanguard

In the early days, graffiti on abandoned structures was often dismissed as mere vandalism. However, as the years rolled on, the artistic community and the general public began to appreciate the transformative power of these urban murals. In the hallowed halls of forgotten stations, a burst of color emerged, telling stories of resilience, hope, and sometimes, good ol' cheeky fun.

3. Iconic Works on the Rails

The Lady of the Tracks: Nestled in an abandoned station in Paris, a mural showcases a woman draped in early 20th-century attire, waiting, perhaps eternally, for a train that will never arrive.

The Steam-Punk Locomotive: In a sidetrack in Melbourne, a stunning rendition of a futuristic steam train melds the old with the new, echoing the evolving nature of transportation.

4. The Duality of Expression

While many artists use these spaces to showcase their creativity, others use them as platforms for social commentary. In a world that often moves too quickly, these sprawling murals ask us to pause, reflect, and sometimes challenge our perceptions.

5. Festivals and Celebrations

Recognizing the cultural significance of such art, many cities have initiated graffiti festivals. Old rail yards brim with life once again as artists from around the world gather, converting rusty carriages and crumbling platforms into masterpieces.

6. The Debate: Preservation or Erasure?

With the growing appreciation of railway graffiti as an art form, debates ensue. Should these works be preserved as part of the evolving history of the tracks, or should they be cleaned off in the name of conservation? It's a delicate balance between honoring the past and embracing the present.

7. An Unexpected Tourist Attraction

Tour guides with colorful umbrellas, and leading enthusiastic groups with cameras are now a common sight around these artistic hubs. Who would've thought? Abandoned railways, once symbols of industrial decline, have metamorphosed into bustling art galleries under the open sky.

8. Chugging Ahead: The Future of Railway Art

With the advent of modern virtual reality and augmented reality, the next wave of railway art might just be digital. Imagine walking through an old station, smartphone in hand, witnessing art come alive, telling tales of ghost trains and long-forgotten journeys.

In a delightful twist of irony, it's the art of the present that keeps the memories of these silent tracks alive. From spray paints to digital overlays, the abandoned railways continue their journey, not through landscapes, but through the evolving realms of artistic expression. The next time you spot a vibrant mural on a rusty carriage, take a moment. Behind the hues and lines lies a story waiting to be discovered.

CHAPTER 11: TALES FROM THE TRACKS: PERSONAL NARRATIVES FROM RAILWAY WORKERS

Railway stations have long been hubs of human activity, and tracks have carried with them a plethora of memories. Yet, no one knows the pulse of the railways as intimately as those who've worked on them. In this chapter, we'll take a sojourn through time, fueled by the recollections of those who've lived the railway life. All aboard the memory express!

1. The Locomotive Whisperer:

Reginald Thompson, a steam locomotive engineer from the 1950s, recalls, "Each engine had its own soul. You could feel it humming, complaining on a tough ascent, or purring on a smooth stretch. It was as if we communicated, the engine and I, in an unspoken language of steam and coal."

2. Station Stories:

Helen Martinez, a ticket seller in the bustling New York Central Station in its heyday, narrates, "The station was a melting pot. Soldiers are bidding teary farewells, lovers' reunions, and kids on their first big-city adventures. Every ticket I sold was a gateway to a different tale."

3. Midnight Tales and Moonlit Rails:

Night guards have a different tale to tell. George Anderson, who patrolled a secluded station in Scotland, mentions, "The nights were eerily silent, broken only by the hoot of an owl or the distant whirr of an approaching train. There were nights when I felt I wasn't alone but accompanied by the spirits of trains past."

4. The Unseen Heroes:

Railway tracks demanded rigorous maintenance. Jamie Watt, a track repairman, sheds light on this. "We'd be out there in the dead of night, rain or shine, ensuring every bolt and sleeper was in place. The tracks were like a never-ending puzzle, and we, its diligent solvers."

5. The Great Train Chefs:

Yes, trains had their own culinary maestros! Amy Robertson, who once led the kitchen in a luxury train, says, "Our kitchen was ever bustling. We'd whip up delicacies even as the landscape outside changed from snowy peaks to sun-kissed deserts. The challenge was real, but so was the satisfaction."

6. Melodies of the Tracks:

Many stations had their own bands or musicians. Tom O'Reilly, who played the violin at a Dublin station, reminisces, "Music added life to the brick and mortar. We'd play tunes that resonated with the rhythm of arriving and departing trains, creating an unforgettable melody of memories."

7. Lost and Found Chronicles:

Jane Willis, who managed a lost and found booth, chuckles, "You'd be amazed at what people leave behind – from umbrellas to a cage with a parrot that squawked 'Late again!' The station, in many ways, was an endless treasure hunt."

8. Farewell to the Tracks:

As time rolled on and many railways shuttered, workers had to bid adieu. Mike Turner, a veteran conductor, poignantly states, "When the final whistle blew, and the last train chugged away, it wasn't just the end of a journey but the conclusion of countless stories. The tracks might've fallen silent, but the tales... they linger."

Indeed, the heart of the railway isn't just steel and steam but the myriad stories it has nurtured over time. So, the next time you cross a forsaken railway or a dilapidated station, remember it's not just infrastructure; it's a repository of tales waiting to be heard, remembered, and retold.

CHAPTER 12: THE ENVIRONMENTAL IMPACT: NATURE'S RECOVERY AND ENVIRONMENTAL BENEFITS

As the relentless chugging of trains grew silent and the bustling of once-thriving stations faded, a new symphony began to unfold. Nature, in its ever-resilient manner, started reclaiming these deserted realms. Abandoned railways not only offer us a portal to history but also a lesson in ecological restoration and resilience.

1. The Green Takeover:

In places where railways were once the lifelines, flora has sprung to life. From the cracks between sleepers, wildflowers bloom, shrubs extend their branches, and trees cast their shadows. The steel has become a trellis for climbers, and the ballast, a bed for seedlings. It's as if Mother Earth is whispering, "Nature abhors a vacuum."

2. Wildlife Corridors:

Deserted tracks have evolved into unintentional wildlife corridors. Deer meander along forgotten routes, birds nest in the rafters of derelict stations, and small mammals find refuge in the undergrowth. These reclaimed paths have created safe passageways for animals, free from the threats of urban sprawl.

3. Carbon Sequestration:

The vegetation overtaking these tracks plays an unsung hero in the fight against climate change. Plants absorb carbon dioxide, providing a natural mechanism to combat rising atmospheric CO_2 levels. Though the individual contribution might seem trivial, when viewed collectively, these silent tracks make a resounding environmental statement.

4. Water Management:

Many abandoned railways, with their gravel and permeable surfaces, act as natural drainage systems. They aid in groundwater recharge, preventing runoff during heavy rains and reducing the risk of urban floods. Nature, it seems, has turned civil engineer.

5. Urban Green Spaces:

In cities starved for greenery, these reclaimed tracks have become invaluable green lungs. They not only purify the air but also offer serene escapes from the urban hustle. The High Line in New York is a prime example: once a railway relic, now an elevated park providing respite to city dwellers.

6. Biodiversity Boost:

Different species of plants and animals have found homes in these tracks-turned-habitats. The variety of life is staggering—from fungi to foxes. The silent tracks have become hotspots of biodiversity, showcasing nature's capacity to rebound and flourish.

7. Pollution and Soil Remediation:

In some locations, the earth beneath the tracks has absorbed pollutants over the years. Remarkably, certain plants, known as hyperaccumulators, have the ability to absorb and concentrate these pollutants from the soil, effectively purifying the ground they grow in.

8. A Reminder of Sustainability:

While the reclamation by nature is inspiring, these tracks also serve as reminders. They symbolize the cost of relentless industrialization and underscore the importance of sustainable development. If nature can find a way back amidst the steel and stone, surely we can find a way to coexist harmoniously.

To tread on these tracks is to witness a masterclass in resilience and renewal. Nature's artistry in these spaces paints a picture of hope and offers a roadmap for ecological balance. So, the next time you walk along an overgrown railway or sit by a station reclaimed by ivy, take a moment to appreciate the silent environmental symphony playing all around you. It's a melody of restoration, a song of hope, and a ballad of a planet that refuses to give up.

CHAPTER 13: PRESERVING HISTORY: EFFORTS TO PROTECT AND MAINTAIN DESERTED RAILWAYS

As the hands of time sweep forward, our world undergoes a constant metamorphosis, casting aside the old to make way for the new. Yet, within this unstoppable march, there's an enduring charm in remnants of the past that refuse to fade into obscurity. Deserted railways, with their tales of ambition, romance, and sometimes tragedy, are treasures waiting to be rediscovered. Though they've fallen silent, the echoes of their stories persist, urging us to preserve and cherish them.

1. The Fight Against Time and Elements:

Wood rots, metal corrodes, and nature incessantly tries to reclaim. Yet, there are organizations and passionate individuals working tirelessly to combat these forces, ensuring that the railway lines and stations retain their age-old glory. Restoring a railway is like fighting a duel with time - and some enthusiastic souls are up for the challenge!

2. Railway Museums: Where Trains Never Retire:

Across the globe, several museums have sprung up dedicated to the romance of rail. Here, abandoned engines and carriages get a fresh lease on life, reminding visitors of the luxurious Orient Express or the humble local service that once chugged through sleepy towns.

3. Recognition as Heritage Sites:

Many governments and international bodies are recognizing the historical significance of these tracks. Designating them as heritage sites not only ensures protection but also promotes them as tourism hotspots. After all, who can resist the allure of walking down a track laden with stories?

4. Adopt a Station:

There are fascinating 'Adopt a Station' schemes where communities or individuals take responsibility for an abandoned station's upkeep. Like adopting a pet, but less furry and more historical.

5. Digital Documentation:

In the digital age, many enthusiasts have turned to platforms like blogs, vlogs, and virtual tours to document and share the grandeur of these forgotten sites. They may be silent in the physical world, but online, they're making quite the noise!

6. Artistic Resurrection:

Art has a beautiful way of reviving memories. From murals that capture the essence of a bygone era to theatre productions staged in old stations, art is ensuring that the legacy of these tracks lives on vibrantly.

7. Educational Outreach:

Schools and colleges are introducing students to the world of abandoned railways, hoping to instill an appreciation for history and engineering. Field trips to deserted tracks? Now that's a class many would eagerly attend!

8. Festivals and Events:

What better way to celebrate these railways than with festivities? Be it vintage train exhibitions, historical reenactments, or simply a picnic on an old platform; these events breathe life back into desolate tracks.

9. Merchandise and Memorabilia:

From scale models of old trains to T-shirts proclaiming love for a particular deserted route, merchandise keeps the spirit of the railways alive and chugging, one souvenir at a time.

10. Grassroots Movements:

Local communities often come together, voicing concerns over potential demolitions or neglect of old railways. Their love for these tracks, punctuated by protests, petitions, and awareness drives, is a testament to the deep-rooted connections many have with these railways.

While these railways may have reached the end of their functional journey, their stories are far from over. Thanks to the combined efforts of governments, communities, and railway enthusiasts, the rich tapestry of memories woven around these tracks remains vivid. As we stroll down an old platform or marvel at a rusting locomotive, let's tip our hats to those ensuring that the past, with its grandeur and lessons, is preserved for generations to come. Because, in the words of a certain witty historian, "History might be old, but it's far from outdated!"

CHAPTER 14: THE ALLURE OF URBAN EXPLORATION: RISKS AND REWARDS

Urban exploration, affectionately dubbed 'Urbex,' has captivated adventurers across the globe for decades. There's a magnetic pull to the hidden, the forgotten, and the off-limits, making abandoned railways prime targets for these modern-day Indiana Joneses (minus the bullwhip and fedora, of course).

1. The Siren Song of Forsaken Rails:

Just what is it about deserted tracks that lure explorers in? The thrill of unearthing forgotten stories, of capturing ghostly stations in their lens, or simply the allure of wandering where few dare tread. Each creak of an old train car, every rusted bolt and rail, promises a tale waiting to be told.

2. Packing the Essentials:

The Urbex community has a credo: "Take nothing but photographs, leave nothing but footprints." With camera gear, torches, sturdy boots, and often a healthy supply of sandwiches (because adventuring is hungry work!), explorers are well-prepared for their jaunts into railway history.

3. The Rewards: Unparalleled Perspectives

There's a certain reward in seeing the world from forgotten platforms, in imagining the bustling crowds and now hearing nothing but echoes. The mosaic of nature, intertwined with remnants of human endeavor, presents a tableau that few get to witness.

4. The Unexpected Finds:

From old ticket stubs dating back decades to forgotten love letters, the gems unearthed during these excursions offer a tantalizing glimpse into a world long gone. And let's not forget the occasional rodent or bird making a surprise cameo!

5. Dangers Lurking in the Shadows:

But with rewards come risks. Dilapidated structures, hidden pits, or even a stray wild animal could turn an adventure into a perilous endeavor. And let's not even mention the potential for a surprise rendezvous with security personnel or, perhaps, a disgruntled ghost conductor.

6. Ethics and Respect:

While exploration offers thrilling escapades, there's a strong undercurrent of respect within the community. Desecrating sites or leaving a mess in one's wake is frowned upon. After all, these sites, in their haunting stillness, command reverence.

7. Sharing the Eerie Beauty:

Thanks to social media, explorers can share their findings with a global audience. Instagram, in particular, has seen a surge in hauntingly beautiful photographs of abandoned railways, cementing their place in modern digital folklore.

8. Bonds Forged on Tracks:

Explorers often band together in groups, forging lasting friendships on their expeditions. There's camaraderie in shared adventure and the occasional shared misadventure (like that time with the owl in the old signal box!).

9. A Word of Caution:

While the pull of exploration is strong, it's vital to understand the risks involved. Many seasoned Urbex practitioners emphasize the importance of safety, awareness, and always letting someone know where you're headed.

10. The Endless Journey:

For every railway explored, countless remain, beckoning with their silent allure. The quest to document, understand, and marvel at these remnants is an endless journey, one that promises to captivate generations of explorers.

In the hush of deserted tracks, as explorers tread lightly, camera in hand, heart aflutter, there's a whispered promise of adventure, of stories untold. And while the trains may no longer run, the spirit of discovery is alive and well, ensuring that these tracks, in their silent majesty, continue to see footprints of those enchanted by their lore. As they say in the Urbex world, "Adventure is just a rusted rail away!"

CHAPTER 15: CINEMATIC RAILS: ABANDONED RAILWAYS IN FILM AND TELEVISION

Railways have always had a romance about them, an undeniable blend of nostalgia, technological marvel, and human stories. The silver screen, ever the preserver of life's grand spectacles, has ensured that the tales of these steel serpents never fade. But it's not just the grand operational railways that Hollywood has a soft spot for. The quiet, deserted tracks and stations have often played muse to many a filmmaker.

1. Setting the Scene:

Nothing screams 'atmospheric' quite like a disused railway track, overrun with the tendrils of nature. It's an immediate visual metaphor - of times gone by, of humanity's transience. Such a location sets the tone without a word of dialogue.

2. The Eerie Suspense:

Think of any psychological thriller, and there's often a scene of a protagonist wandering the silent tracks, heart pounding, as the audience sits on the edge of their seats. "Where are they? Where does the track lead?" The inherent mystery of abandoned railways can heighten suspense like few other settings can.

3. Romantic Rails:

Then there's the romance. Two characters, separated by fate, meet on an old platform, surrounded by memories. There's a bittersweet tinge to these scenes, blending the sadness of lost time with the beauty of the present.

4. Post-apocalyptic Landscapes:

Abandoned railways have also perfectly fit the post-apocalyptic genre. They showcase a world where the hustle and bustle have vanished, leaving behind eerie silences and stark reminders of what once was.

5. Blockbusters that Banked on Tracks:

Several critically acclaimed films have utilized the haunting charm of deserted railways. Take, for example, the post-apocalyptic world depicted in 'The Road' or the thrilling sequences in 'Stand by Me,' where kids walk along a deserted track, each rail leading them closer to adulthood.

6. T.V. Series with a Twist:

Beyond the big screen, television series have also leveraged the atmospheric essence of abandoned rails. They've become the backdrop for character introspections, action-packed sequences, or even supernatural shenanigans.

7. Silent Stories of Silent Tracks:

Documentaries, too, have captured the silent tales of these railways. Through in-depth interviews, breathtaking visuals, and historical recounts, viewers are transported to the heyday of these tracks, feeling the silent weight of their decline.

8. Behind the Scenes:

But filming in these locations isn't a cakewalk. Production teams often grapple with unpredictable terrains, structural safety concerns, and the challenge of bringing equipment to such remote spots. Yet, the resulting cinematic brilliance often makes the toil worth it.

9. The Importance of Authenticity:

Digital effects have made recreating any setting a possibility. However, purist filmmakers still vouch for the authenticity that real locations bring. The nuances of a real abandoned station, with its rusted signs and aged platforms, are hard to replicate.

10. Inspiring Future Generations:

Cinema has the power to immortalize. While many abandoned railways might further degrade or get repurposed, their cinematic avatars will remain, reminding future generations of their glorious past.

Film and television, in their eternal quest for captivating stories and settings, have found consistent allies in abandoned railways. They not only provide the atmospheric depth that filmmakers crave but also ensure that these silent tracks continue to echo in the annals of cinematic history. And who knows? The next time you find yourself enthralled by a riveting scene set against the backdrop of rusted tracks and overgrown platforms, you might just recognize it from your own silent railway adventures! Lights, camera, and tracks!

CHAPTER 16: PHOTOGRAPHIC JOURNEYS: CAPTURING THE ESSENCE OF GHOST TRAINS

As the saying goes, "A picture is worth a thousand words." But when it comes to photographing abandoned railways, it's worth adding that every image captures a thousand memories, a thousand stories, and a thousand dreams left behind. In this chapter, we'll take you through the lens of photographers who've dedicated their art to the silent tracks and their timeless allure.

1. Through the Lens: The Power of Stillness:

A still photograph of a deserted railway track, with rails winding into the horizon, might seem quiet, but the story it tells is anything but silent. The rust on the rails, the overgrowth sneaking its way up the sleepers, and the vacant platforms all speak of times past, vibrant histories, and the inexorable passage of time.

2. The Golden Hour on Rusty Tracks:

Every photographer will vouch for the magic of the golden hour —the short time just after sunrise or before sunset. The soft gold light lends an ethereal glow to the rusted tracks and dilapidated stations, creating images that are both haunting and captivating.

3. Black and White: Amplifying Nostalgia:

There's something profoundly poignant about black-and-white photographs of abandoned places. The monochromatic tones accentuate the contrast of past and present, creating an almost palpable sense of nostalgia.

4. Playing with Perspective:

Some photographers lie flat on the ground, capturing the tracks from below, making them look like they stretch on for an eternity. Others perch themselves high up, showcasing the expanse of the tracks as they carve their way through the landscapes.

5. Portraits Amidst Ruins:

Humans add a touch of life to these dormant tracks. A lone figure standing at a platform, waiting for a train that will never come, or a couple walking hand in hand down a moss-covered rail line, lends a fresh perspective on the tales these tracks hold.

6. Capturing the Elements:

Rain-soaked platforms, snow-covered rail lines, tracks glistening under a summer sun, or stations shrouded in autumn mist – the changing elements add a dynamic dimension to these static, silent places.

7. Chasing Ghost Trains:

While the trains might have long ceased their journeys on these tracks, in the eyes of many photographers, they still live on. With a play of light, shadow, and long exposure techniques, some manage to recreate the ghostly presence of trains, turning photos into ethereal artworks.

8. Behind the Shot: The Challenges:

But photographing abandoned railways isn't as simple as point-and-shoot. There are challenges - accessing some of these remote locations, ensuring safety, and sometimes even having to deal with unfriendly wildlife or unpredictable weather. Yet, ask any photographer, and they'll tell you the final shot is worth every hiccup.

9. The Ethical Side of Photography:

With the surge in interest in urban exploration and railway photography, there's a rising need to discuss ethics. Capturing the beauty without causing harm, respecting the place, and not disturbing any elements are key principles that responsible photographers adhere to.

10. A Portal to the Past:

Every photograph of an abandoned railway is more than just an image. It's a doorway, a portal that transports viewers back in time, letting them hear the distant chugging of engines, the laughter of passengers, and the timeless tales of tracks that once connected souls.

Photography is art, storytelling, and history all rolled into one. And when the subject is something as evocative as abandoned railways, the results are nothing short of magic. So the next time you stumble upon a photograph of a silent track or a deserted station, take a moment. Look closer. There's a story there waiting to be heard, seen, and felt.

CHAPTER 17: THE ROLE OF POLITICS: GOVERNMENT DECISIONS AND THEIR CONSEQUENCES FOR RAILWAYS

When you stand at the edge of a deserted railway platform or tread lightly upon rusty tracks, it's easy to get lost in romanticized tales of bygone eras. But, as the sagely urban planner and occasional train enthusiast Penny T. Wise once quipped, "Behind every abandoned track, there's a trail of paperwork." Indeed, while natural events, technological advances, and changing economies played their roles in the decline of many railways, political decisions often sealed their fates.

1. Nationalization and Its Impacts:

Across the globe, governments grappled with the decision to nationalize or privatize railways. In some regions, nationalization streamlined and saved ailing railways. In others, it meant prioritizing certain lines over others, leaving many tracks destined for silence.

2. Prioritizing Highways over Byways:

The mid-20th century saw the rise of the automobile, and governments were keen to invest in expansive highway networks. Railways, especially those running through rural areas, often got the short end of the budget stick.

3. The Beeching Axe – A British Tale:

Dr. Richard Beeching's name might be muttered with a certain amount of... dismay among U.K. rail enthusiasts. Commissioned to make the railways profitable again, his report led to the closure of thousands of stations and much of the rail network, leaving many towns rail-less and many tracks lifeless.

4. Urbanization and Its Discontents:

With more people flocking to the cities, governments worldwide were often more eager to fund urban transport projects. Thus, many regional and suburban rail lines, once the lifelines of smaller towns, found themselves on the political chopping block.

5. The Environmental Angle:

While abandoned tracks might seem like a loss, many governments were ahead of their time in realizing the environmental benefits. Unused tracks, left untouched, often turned into green corridors, home to flora and fauna, making them the accidental environmentalists of the urban world.

6. Funding Dilemmas and Economic Crises:

During times of economic downturn, maintenance and operation of lesser-used railways were often viewed as expendable expenditures. Fiscal frugality sometimes took precedence over the romance of the rails.

7. The Transition to High-Speed Rail:

As technology progressed, so did the dream of high-speed trains. With speed came the need for specialized tracks, rendering many older tracks obsolete, much like asking a vintage typewriter to run the latest software.

8. The Double-Edged Sword of Heritage Preservation:

While many governments recognized the historical value of old railways and launched efforts to preserve them, some, inadvertently or otherwise, stymied revival projects with red tape and bureaucratic hurdles.

9. The Pull of Progress:

On some occasions, abandoned railway land, especially in urban areas, was seen as prime real estate. Re-zoning for commercial or residential use sometimes proved more lucrative than reviving a dormant rail line.

10. The Quiet Revolutions:

Yet, it wasn't all gloom and doom. Many communities, in the face of government decisions, rallied together to keep their railways alive, even if it meant transitioning them into walking trails, museums, or community spaces.

While nature, time, and progress have played their parts, political choices have shaped the destinies of many a railway. As we stroll down these silent tracks, it's essential to remember that they are not just remnants of engineering marvels but also the outcomes of policy decisions, strategic choices, and, sometimes, a good dash of bureaucratic befuddlement. So, next time you find an old rail ticket or a rusty spike, remember it's not just a piece of history; it's a piece of political legacy.

CHAPTER 18: RAILWAY GHOST TOWNS: COMMUNITIES BUILT AND DISSOLVED AROUND TRAINS

All aboard the memory express!

When we think of railways, it's natural to visualize the chugging locomotives, the hustle-bustle of stations, or the serene landscapes flashing past a window. But, often forgotten, nestled in the shadows of these colossal structures and moving machines, are the communities that sprang up, thrived, and sometimes faded away with the rise and fall of the railway tide. Welcome to the ghost towns: places where the whistle of a train once signified life and prosperity but is now replaced by the haunting hush of history.

1. Rise of the Railroad Towns:

The late 19th and early 20th centuries saw a railway boom. And with it, like mushrooms after the rain, towns popped up. They sprouted around stations, rail yards, and junctions, thriving on the business the railways brought in.

2. Once Prosperous, Now Silent:

Take, for instance, the legendary story of Promontory, Utah. Here, the Golden Spike was driven, connecting the Central Pacific and Union Pacific Railroads. The event turned Promontory into a bustling hub, but today? Crickets (and a nifty museum)!

3. Jobs on Wheels:

Railway towns didn't just rely on the passengers. They were homes to countless railway workers—drivers, guards, signalmen, and maintenance crews. When rail lines shut down or rerouted, jobs disappeared, and so did the townsfolk.

4. Ghostly Remnants:

In some of these towns, while the people may have moved on, they left behind remnants of their lives. Deserted homes, schools, and local businesses stand as silent witnesses to livelier days.

5. The Disappearing Act:

Not all railway towns faded away completely. Some transformed, adapting to new industries or becoming historical sites or tourist attractions. Others? They vanished off the map, leaving behind just a name and tales passed down generations.

6. Cultural Hubs Turned Ghostly Abodes:

Railway towns were often cultural melting pots. Festivals, fairs, and local markets made them vibrant and lively. Today, in some deserted towns, you might still find a dilapidated stage where once local bands played or a town square where dances and celebrations occurred.

7. The Few Lucky Ones:

There were, however, some towns resilient to change. When railways bid them goodbye, they found new lifelines, maybe in the form of highways, local attractions, or by preserving their rich history.

8. Tourism: A Second Life?

The mystique of a ghost town is undeniable. Many former railway towns are now popular tourist spots. They offer a nostalgic trip back in time for the curious souls, where every brick and stone has a tale to whisper.

9. Lessons from the Past:

The rise and fall of these towns teach us about adaptability, resilience, and the impermanence of life. They're stark reminders that change is the only constant.

10. A Respectful Visit:

If you ever find yourself wandering in one of these ghost towns, tip your hat (literal or metaphorical) to the memories. Walk gently, for you tread on dreams, ambitions, love stories, and farewells.

In essence, the saga of railway ghost towns is not just about abandoned buildings or silent tracks. It's about human aspirations, community spirit, and the ever-changing wheels of time. So, next time you chance upon a forgotten railway sign or a moss-covered station, pause for a moment. Close your eyes, and you might just hear the echoes of laughter, the distant chug of a train, and feel the pulse of a town that once was.

CHAPTER 19:
FUTURE PROSPECTS:
POTENTIAL REUSES
FOR ABANDONED
TRACKS AND
STATIONS

Choo-Choo-Choose to Reuse! All aboard the innovation express, where we'll explore the potential rebirth of the silent tracks and stations.

As the adage goes, one person's trash is another person's treasure. The same can be said for abandoned railways. While they may no longer feel the thunderous vibrations of locomotives, these deserted tracks and stations are filled with opportunities just waiting to be seized.

1. Rails to Greenways:

If you've ever fantasized about cycling or jogging on a track without the risk of an oncoming train, you're in luck! Many former railway lines are being transformed into serene paths. Lined with flora and fauna, they're the green lungs of urban landscapes, perfect for nature lovers and fitness enthusiasts alike.

2. Train Stations turned Cafés and Restaurants:

Picture sipping a latte where passengers once waited, the rhythmic sound of steam replaced by smooth jazz. Some disused stations have embraced their history and morphed into themed eateries, where every dish comes with a side of nostalgia.

3. Boutique Hotels with a Story:

Rest your head where once rested, well, freight? Old stations and even carriages are being renovated into boutique hotels. Luxury amidst history; it's like sleeping in a museum – but with better bedding.

4. Community Centers on the Track:

Many old stations have spacious interiors, making them ideal for community events. Art exhibitions, farmers' markets, and even yoga classes have found homes here, bringing life back to these old platforms.

5. Sustainable Urban Farms:

Vertical farming and hydroponics are on the rise. Old railway yards, with their expansive spaces, are perfect for such ventures. From farm to table, all within city limits, reducing the carbon footprint one rail at a time.

6. Theatrical Stages:

Who needs Broadway or West End when you've got Platform 9¾? These grand, cavernous stations provide an atmospheric backdrop for plays and musicals. The acoustics? Well, they're just the ticket!

7. Pop-Up Retail Spaces:

From vintage flea markets to indie bookstores, the old waiting rooms and platforms can be an entrepreneur's dream. The architecture provides a unique shopping experience, with each purchase echoing tales of yesteryears.

8. Museums and Educational Centers:

Some communities choose to celebrate their railway heritage by transforming old stations into museums. They preserve the magic of steam and steel while educating younger generations about the golden age of rail travel.

9. Urban Housing with a Twist:

Space is a premium in cities. Repurposing old carriages and stations into living quarters? It's not only practical but also incredibly stylish. A loft with a train view, anyone?

10. Coworking Spaces for the Modern Nomad:

In our digital age, work is no longer confined to cubicles.

Old stations offer vast spaces, perfect for collaborative working environments, networking hubs, or just a quiet spot to pen your next novel.

11. Parks and Recreational Areas:

Some communities opt to preserve the green around the rails, turning them into public parks. Kids playing where trains once chugged, talk about a role reversal!

In essence, while the clamor and clangor of trains may be a thing of the past for these tracks and stations, their potential is limitless. They stand as testaments to history, ready to be imbued with new purpose. So the next time you spot an abandoned track or station, don't just see a relic; envision its vibrant future.

CHAPTER 20:
SAFETY MEASURES:
PRECAUTIONS FOR
RAILWAY EXPLORERS

If you've made it to this chapter, there's a good chance you've been thoroughly entranced by the tales and visuals of abandoned railways. And perhaps, just perhaps, you're entertaining the idea of embarking on your own railway exploration adventure. But wait! Before you don those hiking boots and arm yourself with a camera, let's take a pit stop at the safety station. Because, let's face it, ghostly encounters aside, these abandoned railways can be filled with very real dangers.

1. Knowledge is Power (and Safety):

Before heading out, research the location thoroughly. Know the history, understand the terrain, and be aware of any known hazards or off-limits areas. Forums and local historical societies can be invaluable in this regard.

2. Buddy Up:

Never go exploring alone. Take a friend, or better yet, a group. A 'track buddy' isn't just fun; they are a literal lifesaver in the event of emergencies.

3. Dress the Part:

Wear sturdy shoes. Abandoned railways might have broken glass, rusty nails, or uneven tracks. Also, dress in layers, and ensure you're visible with bright clothing or a reflective vest.

4. Headgear Heroes:

A good-quality helmet can protect you from low-hanging obstacles or the occasional bump when navigating through old train carriages or stations.

5. Illuminate the Unknown:

Always bring a flashlight, even during the day. Train tunnels or station basements can plunge you into darkness unexpectedly.

6. Be Alert to Your Surroundings:

It's easy to be enthralled by the eerie beauty and forget to watch your step. Stay aware, particularly around platforms or near any open pits.

7. No Trespassing (Really!):

Obey all signage. If an area says 'No Entry,' respect it. It's there for a reason. Remember, trespassing isn't just illegal; it can be dangerous.

8. Steer Clear of Wildlife:

While flora might have taken over, fauna isn't far behind. Watch out for animals, snakes, or even nesting birds. Remember, it's their home now.

9. Update Someone:

Always inform someone about your exploration plans, including the location and expected return time. This way, if things go south, someone knows where to start looking.

10. Emergency Prep is Essential:

Carry a basic first aid kit, whistle, water, snacks, and a fully charged phone. The signal might be weak or non-existent, so consider investing in a GPS beacon.

11. Historical Respect:

These railways are historical sites. While it might be tempting to take a 'souvenir,' leave everything as you found it. Take pictures, not artifacts.

12. Physical Limits are Real:

Don't push yourself too hard. If an area seems inaccessible or too dangerous, it's okay to turn back. Live to explore another day!

In the excitement of adventure, it's easy to forget that the railways, despite their silence, still have stories to tell and secrets to keep. Respect them, protect yourself, and ensure your railway exploration tale is one of awe and thrill, not of cautionary tales.

Happy (and safe) exploring, intrepid traveler!

CHAPTER 21: REBIRTH AND REVIVAL: STORIES OF DESERTED RAILWAYS BROUGHT BACK TO LIFE

If you've been with us from the start, you've ventured through the echoes, myths, and mysteries surrounding abandoned railways. Now, it's time to steer the narrative towards a hopeful horizon, where some deserted tracks have been given a second lease on life. Think of them as phoenixes, rising from the ashen memories of yesteryears, breathing new life into communities and landscapes.

1. From Rails to Green Trails:

Many old railway tracks have found reincarnation as walking, jogging, or cycling trails. The High Line in New York City, once a freight rail line that was raised above the streets of Manhattan, is a prime example. Today, it stands transformed into an urban oasis, buzzing with plant life, art, and, most importantly, people.

2. Commuter Revival:

Several old railways, especially those near bustling cities, have been modernized and reintegrated into the city's public transportation system. A nod to efficiency and sustainability, they've become essential arteries once more, albeit with electric trains instead of steam.

3. Tourism Transitions:

What was once a forsaken track in Wales has now turned into the world-famous Ffestiniog Railway, a heritage railway that attracts tourists year-round. Chugging along in vintage carriages, passengers are treated to the kind of scenic beauty that only a train journey can offer.

4. Platforms of Art and Culture:

Some disused stations have been converted into cultural hubs —art galleries, music venues, or theaters. They serve as venues where the echoes of passing trains complement the rhythm of music and the vibrancy of art.

5. Dining on the Line:

There's something undeniably romantic about dining in a vintage railway carriage. Several entrepreneurs have tapped into this charm by turning old carriages and stations into themed restaurants or cafes. From fine dining to cozy tea rooms, the ambiance echoes tales of bygone eras.

6. The Train Staycation:

Who said trains always need to be on the move? From the Netherlands to Australia, stationary train carriages have been repurposed into unique accommodation options. A delightful blend of nostalgia and comfort, they're a hit amongst travelers seeking offbeat experiences.

7. Sustainable Solutions:

In some places, the infrastructure of old railways is being used for innovative solutions to contemporary problems. For instance, in parts of Europe, old tunnels are considered for mushroom farming, and deserted stations as urban farms, capitalizing on the unique, controlled environments these spaces offer.

8. Museums and Heritage Centers:

Some tracks and stations, bearing significant historical weight, have been preserved as museums. They stand as testimonies to the evolution of rail transport, showcasing everything from antique locomotives to ticket stubs.

9. Industrial Reimagining:

Certain rail yards, with their expansive spaces, have been transformed into industrial parks or innovation hubs, fostering new-age businesses and startups.

So, while it might seem that a deserted railway has reached the end of its journey, it's heartwarming to know that for many, it's just a bend, not the end. With creativity, vision, and a sprinkle of nostalgia, these iron pathways are reborn, proving that sometimes, the past doesn't fade; it simply finds a new track.

Next stop? Fresh beginnings and imaginative revivals!

CHAPTER 22: FAREWELL TO THE SILENT TRACKS: REFLECTING ON THE LEGACY OF ABANDONED RAILWAYS

If train tracks were to have a language of their own, the tales etched into the rusting rails and aging sleepers would be an anthology of human experiences - moments of joy, whispers of farewells, the hustle of daily commuters, and the sighs of solitary travelers. Every abandoned railway, with its silent echoes, embodies this poetic chronicle.

1. Time's Relentless March:

The railways we've traveled through these pages are monuments to progress, innovation, and human ambition. But they also symbolize the inexorable march of time and the ever-evolving nature of society. As horses gave way to steam and steam yielded to electricity, the technology, economics, and politics of the day shaped the fate of these tracks.

2. Remnants of Love Stories:

While our main focus has been on the physical aspects of these abandoned railways, imagine the countless stories of love that these rails have witnessed. From stolen glances between strangers sharing a compartment to tearful farewells on platforms, railways have often been the silent witnesses to the beginnings and ends of countless romances.

3. Platforms of Opportunity:

For many, trains symbolized new beginnings. Be it a youngster leaving his hometown for the first time in search of opportunities, or immigrants catching their first glimpse of a new land from a train window, the railways were, and continue to be, platforms of dreams and aspirations.

4. Environmental Tapestry:

The railways, in their prime, often intruded upon nature, cutting through forests and spanning rivers. In their abandonment, nature reclaims them, creating a unique blend of industrial decay and natural rejuvenation. The moss-covered tracks and the flower-bedecked platforms remind us of nature's persistence.

5. A Whispered Lullaby:

The sounds associated with railways – the rhythmic chugging of engines, the whistles, and the murmurs of passengers – once filled the air. Now, the silence is profound but not absolute. Instead, these tracks resonate with a whispered lullaby of memories.

6. The Future and Beyond:

As we've seen in the chapter about revival, while many tracks lay dormant, others find new purpose. Their resilience serves as a lesson. Nothing is truly abandoned if it holds a place in collective memory or if it can be reimagined for the future.

7. In Gratitude to the Rails:

To truly appreciate the legacy of these deserted railways, one must also recognize the countless individuals who dedicated their lives to them. From the engineers and construction workers to the ticket collectors and tea vendors, railways were ecosystems of human endeavor.

In Summation:

Our journey through the silent tracks has been one of reflection, discovery, and a deep dive into the annals of history. As this chapter comes to a close, remember that every rusted nail, every crumbling platform, and every overgrown path tells a story. It's up to us to listen, learn, and keep the legacy of these tracks alive in our hearts.

And while we may say 'farewell' to these tracks, let's never forget the indelible mark they've left on our shared human journey. After all, tracks might end, but their stories? They're forever.

THE END

Made in the USA
Monee, IL
02 November 2023

45689172R00046